little book of
christenings

little book of
christenings
creative ideas for a special day

beverley jollands

southwater

This edition is published by Southwater

Southwater Books is an imprint of
Anness Publishing Limited
Hermes House
88-89 Blackfriars Road
London SE1 8HA

© Anness Publishing Limited 1999, 2003

This edition distributed in the UK by The Manning Partnership
Ltd, 6 The Old Dairy, Melcombe Road, Bath BA2 3LR;
tel. 01225 478 444; fax 01225 478 440;
sales@manning-partnership.co.uk

This edition distributed in the USA and Canada by National Book
Network, 4720 Boston Way, Lanham, MD 20706;
tel. 301 459 3366; fax 301 459 1705; www.nbnbooks.com

This edition distributed in Australia by Pan Macmillan Australia,
Level 18, St Martins Tower, 31 Market St, Sydney, NSW 2000;
tel. 1300 135 113; fax 1300 135 103;
customer.service@macmillan.com.au

This edition distributed in New Zealand by The Five Mile Press
(NZ) Ltd, PO Box 33–1071 Takapuna, Unit 11/101–111 Diana
Drive, Glenfield, Auckland 10;
tel. (09) 444 4144; fax (09) 444 4518; fivemilenz@clear.net.nz

A CIP catalogue record for this book is available from the British
Library.

Publisher: **Joanna Lorenz**
Editorial Manager: **Helen Sudell**
Designer: **Lisa Tai**
Contributors: **Fiona Barnett, Lucinda Ganderton,
Isabel Stanley, Dorothy Wood**
Photographers: **Debbie Patterson, Michelle Garrett, Lucy
Mason, Peter Williams**
Illustrator: **Lucinda Ganderton**

Previously published as *Christenings a Celebration*

10 9 8 7 6 5 4 3 2 1

Contents

Christening Traditions

Take Thy Child into Thy Care

Who hath not owned, with rapture-smitten frame,

The power of grace, the magic of a name?

Thomas Campbell (1777-1844), *The Pleasures of Hope*

St Mark

And they brought unto him little children, that he should touch them: and the disciples rebuked them. But when Jesus saw it, he was moved with indignation, and said unto them, Suffer the little children to come unto me; forbid them not: for of such is the kingdom of God. Verily I say unto you, Whosoever shall not receive the kingdom of God as a little child, he shall in no wise enter therein. And he took them in his arms, and blessed them, laying his hands upon them.

St Mark 10, 13-16

Good Wishes

Power of raven be thine,
Power of eagle be thine,
    Power of the Fiann.

Power of storm be thine,
Power of moon be thine,
    Power of sun.

Power of sea be thine,
Power of land be thine,
    Power of heaven.

Goodness of sea be thine,
Goodness of earth be thine,
    Goodness of heaven.

Each day be joyous to thee,
No day be grievous to thee,
    Honour and compassion.

Love of each face be thine,
Death on the pillow be thine,
    Thy Saviour's presence.

Anon., translated from the
Gaelic by Alexander Carmichael
(1832-1912)

Monday's
Child is fair of face,

Tuesday's child is full of grace,

Wednesday's child is full of woe,

Thursday's child has far to go,

Friday's child is loving and giving,

Saturday's child works hard for a living,

But the child that is born on the Sabbath day

Is bonny, and blithe, and good, and gay.

Anon.

A Letter to the Child

Lady Margaret Cavendish Holles-Harley

My noble, lovely, little Peggy,
Let this my First Epistle beg ye,
At dawn of morn, and close of even,
To lift your heart and hands to Heaven.
In double beauty say your prayer:
"Our Father" first, then "Notre Père".
And, dearest child, along the day,
In every thing you do and say,
Obey and please my lord and lady,
So God shall love and angels aid ye.

If to these precepts you attend,
No second letter need I send,
And so I rest your constant friend.

Matthew Prior (1664-1721)

Choosing a Name

I have got a new-born sister;
I was nigh the first that kissed her.
When the nursing woman brought her
To papa, his infant daughter,
How papa's dear eyes did glisten! -
She will shortly be to christen:
And papa has made the offer,
I shall have the naming of her.

Now I wonder what would please her,
Charlotte, Julia, or Louisa.
Ann and Mary, they're too common;
Joan's too formal for a woman;
Jane's a prettier name beside;
But we had a Jane that died.
They would say, if 'twas Rebecca,
That she was a little Quaker.
Edith's pretty, but that looks
Better in old English books;
Ellen's left off long ago;
Blanche is out of fashion now.
None that I have named as yet
Are so good as Margaret.
Emily is neat and fine.
What do you think of Caroline?
How I'm puzzled and perplexed
What to choose or think of next!
I am in a little fever,
Lest the name that I shall give her
Should disgrace her or defame her,
I will leave papa to name her.

Charles (1775-1834) and Mary (1764-1847) Lamb

Septuagesima Sunday,

St Valentine's Eve, 1870

Went to Bettws in the afternoon wrapped in two waistcoats, two coats, a muffler and a mackintosh, and was not at all too warm. Heard the Chapel bell pealing strongly for the second time since I have been here and when I got to the Chapel my beard moustaches and whiskers were so stiff with ice that I could hardly open my mouth and my beard was frozen on to my mackintosh. There was a large christening party from Llwyn Gwilym. The clerk (Wilding) thrust a tallow candle between the bars of the stove grate lighted it and set it upon the table that once probably did duty for a Communion table. I had it put out again as the daylight was sufficient. The baby was baptized in ice which was broken and swimming about in the Font.

Rev. Francis Kilvert (1840-1879)

Christening
Customs and Traditions

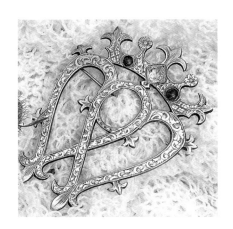

The birth of a baby is a reaffirmation of life for everyone – parents, family and friends – and the ritual of the christening, together with the festivities that follow it, formalizes the welcome that everyone wants to give the new arrival. Although the baby may remain unaware of the fact, this celebration marks his or her first tiny steps into the life of the community.

The Christian sacrament of baptism is similar to the time-honoured customs of many other cultures that welcome a new baby with ceremonial and symbolic purification. In the ancient world, Hebrew, Egyptian and Greek infants all underwent ritual immersion as a symbol of spiritual cleansing. Today, the Jicarillo Indians of Mexico pour water from sacred rivers over the infant's head, while singing to it of the earth's riches.

The early Christian church warned that an unbaptized soul would be stranded forever in limbo,

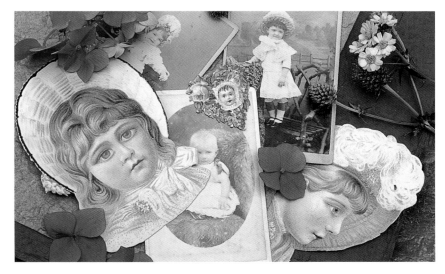

Above: *This double-heart lucky brooch is made from engraved silver and is inlaid with fake gems.*

Left: *A baby album can be compiled to record a child's development and achievements in its first years, and can include other mementoes of childhood.*

so that babies – especially frail ones – had to be baptized immediately to save them from this fate. Although the church's teaching changed, the superstition persisted that baptism brings good luck and that a baby will not thrive until it is named. It was believed that fairies were the spirits of children who had died nameless. In 1685 the diarist John Evelyn noted "a miracle happening in Winchester. . . of a poor miserably sick and decrepit child (as I remember long kept unbaptized) who, immediately on his baptism, recovered".

The christening may be the first occasion on which the baby's Christian names are declared publicly, and it was believed to be unlucky to tell the names beforehand.

Every culture recognizes the power of names, and prospective parents spend hours debating their choices in the hope that a name ringing with admirable qualities will ensure that the child lives up to it.

When the early Christians baptized a baby, it was unclothed and fully submerged in flowing water. If it cried, this was seen as a good omen that would drive out bad spirits. By the seventeenth century, total immersion had been replaced by the symbolic sprinkling of holy water over the baby's head. These days it is usual to baptize babies during a Sunday service. The parents and godparents are asked to affirm their faith on behalf of themselves and the child. After the ceremony everyone gathers to "wet the baby's head" and share the christening cake. Sometimes the cake is the top tier of the parents' wedding cake, a tradition started in the twentieth century, but the eating and drinking is a remnant of the feasting which was intrinsic to the earliest purification rites.

Below: A basket represents the wealth and bounty of the maternal body when given to a new mother and, like the pincushion, is a traditional and useful present.

The Christening Layette

The Needle Plies its Busy Task

Rites, which custom does impose,

Silver bells, and baby clothes.

Charles Lamb (1775-1834)

The Baby Boy

Bless thy full cheeks my noble boy!
God bless thee, thou art all my joy!
May all thy way of life be blest!
Another kiss, and rest thee, rest.
Mayst thou grow to manly prime,
And wed a bride in the primrose time.
Go little moth to my boy's bride,
Seek her out wherever she hide,
Dress her in satin all white and neat,
With a pair of silver bells at her feet!
Set her upon thy silver wings,
Over the shining seas and the springs,
Under the stars and over the corn,
And they'll be here with the peep of morn!

Alfred, Lord Tennyson (1809-1892)

A Special Gown

But here the needle plies its busy task,
The pattern grows, the well-depicted flow'r,
Wrought patiently into the snowy lawn,
Unfolds its bosom; buds and leaves, and sprigs,
And curling tendrils, gracefully dispos'd,
Follow the nimble finger of the fair;
A wreath that cannot fade, of flow'rs that blow
With most success when all besides decay.

William Cowper (1731-1800), from *The Winter Evening*

Christening
Robes

Above: This christening outfit, in silk dupion, would be perfect for a winter baby. It has layers of petticoats, matching bootees and bonnet (top right) and will be kept long after the event.

Up until the seventeenth century, young babies were tightly wrapped in swaddling clothes and carried to the font in a "bearing cloth". This was a large square piece of silk, edged with trimmings of gold lace and braid. The christening robe as we know it today evolved in the mid-eighteenth century, when babies were freed of swaddling at an earlier age. In white silk, the earliest surviving examples have a front opening which was either fastened with ribbon ties or left open to show a petticoat beneath. The decorative curving lines of braid are similar to those applied to women's gowns of the period.

The first christening robes were made in the style worn every day by eighteenth-century children: both boy and girl babies wore "slip" dresses, with a very long, flowing skirt falling from a short, tucked bodice, and a low neck and short sleeves. This fashion has remained popular for christenings ever since. This is partly due to the tradition of handing christening robes down from one generation to the next, so that dozens of babies may wear the same gown over many years. Victorian babies were dressed in gowns decorated with Ayrshire work, a delicate form of white-on-white embroidery that originated in the Scottish Lowlands.

Other items of clothing such as bonnets and bootees could be made to go with the robe. A number of exquisite "christening sets" survive from the seventeenth and eighteenth centuries, including bibs, head bands, mittens and pincushion covers or handkerchiefs in embroidered linen.

If there is no antique gown in your family, create an heirloom for future generations by making a new gown in the finest white or cream lawn or silk, embellished with delicate embroidery, tucking or drawn-thread work. Some families follow the old tradition of saving some of the material used to make the mother's wedding dress, or taking some of the fabric from its train, to make a christening robe.

An old Scottish custom involved pinning a piece of shortbread to the christening robe, to be worn throughout the ceremony. An unmarried girl who ate the shortbread afterwards was sure to dream of her future husband that night. It was also thought essential for the baby to sleep in its christening robe for the first night after baptism, to bring luck and good health in the future.

Right: *Lawn is the finest cotton fabric, and because of its softness has always been used to make baby clothes. This christening dress has intricate embroidery and drawn-thread work, with ribbon to decorate the yoke.*

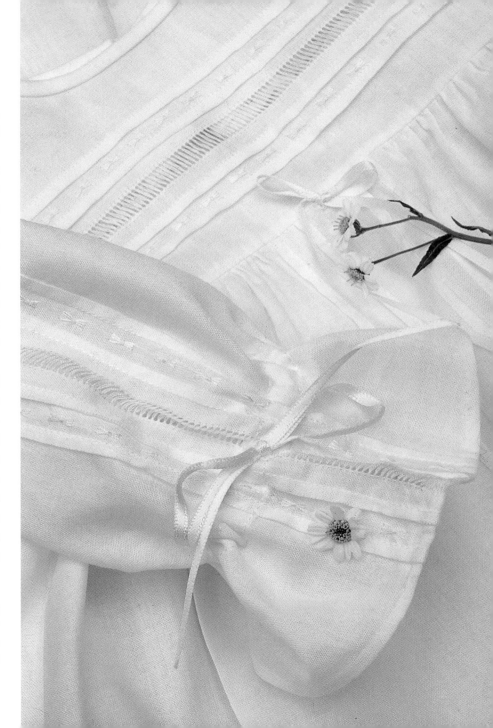

The *Christening* Gown

This classic christening gown is made from fine cream cotton lawn, prettily decorated with cotton lace and tiny seed pearls. Along with a matching bonnet and brocade bootees, it makes a beautiful outfit that is bound to be handed down as a family heirloom.

- paper for pattern
- cream lawn (fine cotton), enough for whole gown
- pins
- scissors
- dressmaker's chalk

- tacking (basting) thread
- needle
- sewing machine
- matching sewing thread
- iron
- 4.5m/5yd cotton lace,

  2cm/¾in wide
- 45cm/18in narrow elastic
- press stud (snap)
- hook and eye
- 2 mother-of-pearl buttons
- seed pearl beads

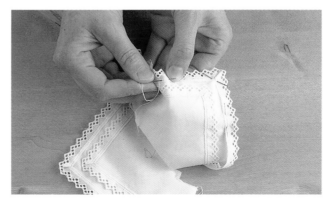

1 Copy the pattern at the back of the book, enlarging to the size required. Lay out all the pieces on the fabric and cut out. Transfer pattern markings. All seam allowances are 1.5cm/⅝in and are finished by zigzagging close to the stitching then trimming. Stitch the right-hand shoulder seam of the collar and the matching seam on the collar facing. Trim the seam allowances to 5mm/¼in and press open.

2 With right sides together, stitch the collar to the facing around three sides, leaving open along the front neck edge. Trim seams, clip corners, turn through the opening and press. Following the markings on the pattern pieces, pin, tack (baste) and stitch the lace in position on the collar and the centre front panel of the skirt, mitring the angles.

3 Stitch the shoulder seams of the yoke and yoke facing, trim the seam allowances to 5mm/¼in and press open. Turn up and press the seam allowance along the lower edges of the yoke facing.

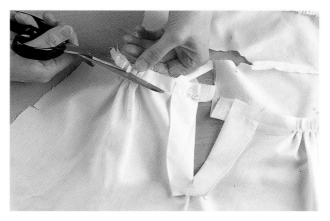

4 Stitch the front side panels to the lace-trimmed centre panel. Join the back seam, ending the stitching at the large dot shown on the pattern. Neaten the edges of the self-facing, fold to the inside and tack (baste) along the top edge. Gather between the notches on the front and back. With right sides together, pin the front and back to the yoke. Adjust the gathers, tack (baste) and stitch. Trim the seam and press towards the yoke.

5 Pin and tack (baste) the collar to the front neck edge of the yoke. Pin and tack (baste) the yoke facing to the yoke, with right sides together.

6 Stitch the yoke and yoke facing together along the centre back and neck edges. Trim seam, clip curves and turn to the right side. Press the yoke facing to the inside. Pin, then slip-stitch along the lower edge. ➤

7 *Turn up 3mm/⅛in along the bottom edge of the sleeve and machine stitch. Trim and turn up again. Pin and tack (baste) the lace on the right side and straight stitch in position.*

8 *Cut out two 30 x 2.5cm/12 x 1in bias strips of lawn. Press in the long edges and stitch to the inside of each sleeve as shown. Thread elastic through these casings and adjust to fit. Stitch securely in place at each end.*

9 *Gather the sleeve head between the notches. Pin and tack (baste) into the armhole, adjusting the gathers. Straight stitch the seam, then zigzag and trim. Stitch the sleeve and side seams. Finish the hem with a lace border as described in Step 7.*

10 *Sew a press stud (snap) to the neck edge of the collar and a hook and eye at the shoulder edge. Make two buttonholes in the right back yoke and sew the mother-of-pearl buttons on the left side. Trim the lace collar with seed pearl beads.*

Right: *This gown has a simple design so that it is comfortable for a baby to wear, but the fine details make it very special.*

Christening Bonnet

This appealing baby bonnet is made from the same fabric as the christening gown, in a co-ordinating style. The peak is finished with matching cotton lace, and the rouleau tie that fastens under the chin is held in place by tiny lace rosettes with seed pearl centres.

- paper for pattern
- cream lawn (fine cotton), enough for whole bonnet
- pins
- scissors
- dressmaker's chalk

- tacking (basting) thread
- needle
- sewing machine
- matching sewing thread
- iron
- 30cm/12in narrow

- elastic
- safety pin
- 50cm/20in cotton lace, 2cm/¾in wide
- seed pearl beads

1 Copy the bonnet pattern at the back of the book, enlarging to the size required. Lay out the pieces on the fabric and cut out. Transfer pattern markings. All seam allowances are 1.5cm / ⅝ in. With right sides together, stitch the two crown pieces together along the straight edge, then stay-stitch around the seam allowance on one piece, trimming and notching to the stitching line.

2 With right sides together, stitch the two main bonnet pieces around the sides and peak, leaving the back edge open. Trim edges and clip corners, turn through and press. Gather the back edge between the dots. Pin and tack (baste) to the crown, matching the dots and adjusting the gathers. Trim the seam and notch the curved edge. Press towards the crown.

3 Pin and tack (baste) the crown facing to the inside of the bonnet. Straight stitch through all layers 5mm / ¼ in from the straight edge of the crown. Thread a length of elastic through this channel. Stitch one end securely, adjust to fit and fasten the other end before trimming. Slip-stitch the facing to the seam around the crown.

4 *Pin and tack (baste) the lace to the underside of the front edge, mitring the corner. Tuck the ends under and stitch.*

5 *Make a rouleau tie from a 40 x 2cm/ 16 x ¾ in bias strip of fabric, joining several pieces if necessary. Fold in half and stitch the long sides together 5mm/¼ in from the fold. Fasten a small safety pin to one end and draw the tube right side out. Press lightly and stitch to each side of the bonnet.*

6 *Make two rosettes from the remaining lace by running a gathering thread along one edge and drawing it up. Decorate with a cluster of seed pearl beads. Sew the rosettes to the bonnet, over the ends of the rouleau tie.*

Right: *The peak of the little bonnet echoes the style of the christening gown, and folds back to frame the baby's face.*

Brocade Bootees

Many mothers treasure their baby's first pair of shoes as a keepsake, and sumptuous brocade bootees would be well worth cherishing. Lined with silk and finished with fine frills and golden tassels, they might well be worn by a fairytale prince or princess.

- paper for pattern
- pins
- scissors
- dressmaker's chalk
- 23 x 90cm/9 x 36in brocade
- 23 x 90cm/9 x 36in lining
- 60cm/24in gold ribbon, 3mm/⅛in wide
- tacking (basting) thread
- needle
- 60cm/24in sheer ribbon, 7.5cm/3in wide
- sewing machine
- matching sewing thread
- iron
- 2 small gold tassels

1 Copy the bootee pattern at the back of the book, enlarging to the size required. Cut two sides, two fronts and two soles from brocade and lining fabrics. Transfer all markings. Cut the gold ribbon into four equal lengths and tack (baste) to the right side of the side pieces at the crosses. Cut the sheer ribbon in half, fold each half lengthways and pin the long edges together. Trim the ends into a curve.

2 Gather the long edges of the sheer ribbon and pin to the right side of the brocade sides between the crosses. Pull up the gathers to fit and tack (baste) in place.

3 Pin the lining and brocade sides together with right sides facing. Stitch along the upper curved edges, taking a 5mm/¼in seam allowance. Snip the seam allowance around the curves and turn through. Press lightly, then tack (baste) the raw edges.

Right: *Opulent golden bootees make a perfect finishing touch for the baby's christening outfit.*

4 Butt the short edges together, matching the dots shown on the pattern, and whip-stitch. With right sides facing, pin the brocade front to the top and the lining front to the underside, matching the dots. Stitch the front seam. Tack (baste) the raw edges of the fronts together with wrong sides facing.

5 Turn to the wrong side. With right sides facing, pin, then tack (baste) the brocade sole to the bootee, matching the notches to the centre front and back seam. Stitch, taking a 5mm/¼in seam allowance. Stitch the lining sole to the bootee, sandwiching the upper part between the soles, and leaving a 5cm/2in gap along a straight edge.

6 Snip the curved edge of the soles, then turn the upper part through to the wrong side. Turn in the raw edge of the lining and slip-stitch the seam closed. Turn to the right side and sew a small gold tassel to the front of each bootee.

Ribbonwork Pillow

This frilled baby pillow combines the freshness of pure white cotton with the silky soft appeal of ribbon embroidery in delicate pastels. Embroidering with narrow ribbon is easy – provided you don't let the ribbon twist too much as you work – and produces a subtly shaded, raised effect.

- 90 × 30cm/36 × 12in white cotton piqué
- scissors
- tape measure
- 23cm/9in square lightweight iron-on interfacing
- iron
- dressmaker's carbon or vanishing marker pen
- embroidery hoop (frame)
- chenille needle

- 2m/2yd satin ribbon, 3mm/¹/₈in wide, in each of the following colours: pale pink, mid-pink, dusky pink, pale mint green, pale lime green, pale aqua
- 1.5m/1¹/₂yd ribbon, 5mm/¹/₄in wide
- 1.5m/1¹/₂yd narrow broderie anglaise insertion
- pins
- sewing machine

- matching sewing thread
- 1.5m/1¹/₂yd broderie anglaise edging, 7.5cm/3in wide
- needle
- tacking (basting) thread
- tapestry needle
- 30 ×30cm/12 × 12in cushion pad

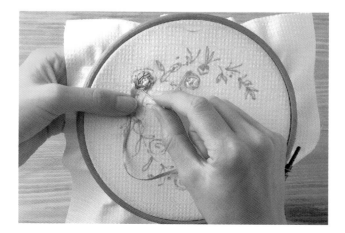

1 Cut a 23cm/9in square of cotton piqué and iron the interfacing to one side. Enlarge the garland design on this page to the required size and transfer to the fabric by tracing it through dressmaker's carbon or by drawing freehand with a vanishing marker pen. Mount the fabric in an embroidery hoop (frame). Work the roses first by stitching a star shape of four overlapping straight stitches in pale pink. With darker pink ribbon, work circles of overlapping stitches around the centre, making the outer stitches slightly longer to give the effect of petals. Work a few more stitches at one side to give depth to the rose.

2 Using the various shades of green ribbon, work the leaves in straight stitch and the rosebuds in lazy daisy stitch. Work a single pink straight stitch for the centre of each rosebud and fill any spaces with small French knots. Work the rest of the garland design using a range of formal and random stitches. The photograph will act as a guide, but need not be followed too rigidly. Trim the finished piece to a 15cm/6in square. Finish with a small, single loop bow made from 5mm/¼in ribbon.

3 Cut four 9cm/3½in squares and four 15 x 9cm/6 x 3½in rectangles of cotton piqué. Cut four 9cm/3½in, two 15cm/6in and two 33cm/13in lengths of broderie anglaise insertion. Using the diagram in the bottom left corner of the page as a guide, edge one side of each square and one long side of two of the rectangles, taking a 1cm/½in seam allowance. Sew the insertion-edged rectangles to opposite sides of the embroidered square. Sew an insertion-edged square to either end of the two remaining rectangles.

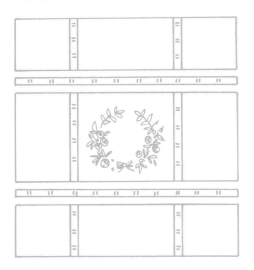

4 Use the two remaining strips of broderie anglaise insertion to join all three strips together, framing the embroidered square. Press the seam allowances towards the central square on the wrong side. ➤

5 Join the two ends of the broderie anglaise edging and run a gathering thread along the raw edge. Fold the edging into four equal sections, marking each quarter division with a small notch. Pin each notch to one corner of the pillow top, right sides together, matching raw edges. Draw up the gathering thread to fit the pillow. Distribute the gathers evenly, allowing a little extra fullness at the corners. Pin, tack (baste) and stitch in place.

6 Thread the 5mm/¼in ribbon through the insertion using a tapestry needle, securing each end with a few stitches.

7 Cut a 30cm/12in square of cotton piqué for the back of the pillow. Pin to the right side of the pillow front, ensuring that the broderie anglaise is free of the seam line. Stitch around three sides. Trim the seams, clip corners and turn through. Insert the cushion pad and slip-stitch the fourth side closed.

Right: A beautiful embroidered pillow will be treasured forever as a memento of the christening.

Baby's Patchwork Quilt

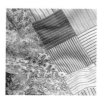

Welcome a new baby into the family circle with this irresistible patchwork quilt. It is made from a harmonious mixture of old and new fabrics, which can be bought or begged from friends and relations. Make sure you use lightweight flameproof wadding (batting) for the filling.

- assortment of striped shirting and floral cottons of similar weight
- iron
- 5cm/2in square template cut from thin card (cardboard)
- pins
- sewing machine (optional)
- matching sewing thread
- needle
- 1m/1yd square backing fabric
- 1m/1yd square lightweight polyester wadding (batting)
- tacking (basting) thread
- quilting thread (if quilting by hand)
- 64 mother-of-pearl buttons (optional)

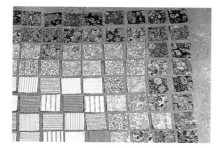

1 Wash all the fabric pieces and press. Using the template, cut out squares following the grain of the fabric. The quilt shown uses 225 in shirting, 136 in light floral fabrics and 168 in dark floral fabrics. Lay out the shirting squares in 15 rows of 15 squares, so that the stripes form a basket-weave pattern. Make up the border with two rows each of light and dark floral squares.

2 Join the squares by hand or machine in units of four, taking a 5mm /¼in seam allowance. Press the seams open and pin each block of four with right sides together, matching the corners. Stitch the blocks together to complete the top of the quilt.

3 Cut the backing fabric and wadding (batting) to the same size as the quilt plus 5cm/2in all round. Sandwich the three layers together, with the cover and backing fabrics right side out. Smooth out the layers and pin together. Tack (baste) all the seams.

Right: *A combination of pink and blue shades makes this patchwork quilt equally suitable for a baby girl or boy.*

4 Quilt by hand or machine, following the seam lines exactly. Stitch along two and four squares in from the edge, and leave three squares between the lines of stitching in the centre panel.

5 Join enough 5cm/2in strips of one of the dark floral fabrics to fit around the outside of the quilt. Press under 1cm/½in along one long edge. With right sides together, matching raw edges, stitch the binding to the quilt 1cm/½in from the edge, mitring the corners. Slip-stitch the folded edge to the backing fabric to enclose the raw edges.

6 If desired, stitch a mother-of-pearl button at each point where the lines of quilting intersect, making sure that they are attached very firmly so that they cannot be pulled off by the child.

Birds and Stars Quilt

This richly coloured quilt is the right size for a Moses basket or small crib. Assemble a collection of fabric scraps with a mixture of prints and weaves so that each appliquéd bird is unique.

- 50 × 90cm/20 × 36in border fabric
- scissors
- sewing machine
- matching sewing thread
- 50 × 65cm/20 × 26in main fabric
- iron
- thin card (cardboard)
- pencil
- craft knife
- assorted fabric scraps, including several shades of green
- pins
- iron-on interfacing
- tissue paper
- tacking (basting) thread
- needle
- 75 × 90cm/30 × 36in polyester wadding (batting)
- 75 × 90cm/30 × 36in backing fabric
- 3.5m/3⅞yd bias binding

1 Cut borders 13cm/5in wide, two 50cm/20in long and two 90cm/36in long. Stitch the short pieces to the shorter sides of the main fabric, taking a 1cm/½in seam allowance, then attach the two longer pieces. Press the seams open. Enlarge the motif templates on this page and make card (cardboard) templates.

2 Select the fabric pieces for the 12 birds, leaves and stars and lay in position on the interfacing. Cover with tissue paper and press: this keeps all the pieces together. Prepare all the birds and cut them out.

3 Arrange the birds on the quilt in three rows of four. Pin, then tack (baste) the pieces in place and secure all the edges with a narrow zigzag stitch.

4 Cut 2cm/¾in wide green bias strips and join to make long strips. Fold in half and stitch 5mm/¼in from the fold. Trim back to the seam line. Press the tubes flat with the stitches underneath.

5 Weave the green strips around the birds to make branches. Pin, then slip-stitch along both edges. Appliqué the leaves to the branches, then fill in the spaces with stars.

6 Sandwich the wadding (batting) between the cover and backing fabric, right sides out, and tack (baste) through all layers. Make the birds' eyes with small stab stitches. Machine stitch around the border seam. Trim the edges. With right sides together, matching raw edges, stitch the binding to the quilt, mitring the corners. Fold the binding to the back and slip-stitch to the backing fabric.

Above: *Delightful naïve birds sitting on twining branches make a bold design for an appliquéd nursery quilt.*

Christening
Gifts

Gifts to Welcome the Baby

Of all nature's gifts to the human race, what

is sweeter to a man than his children?

Marcus Tullius Cicero (106-43 BC)

Sleeping Beauty

There were formerly a king and a queen, who were so sorry that they had no children; so sorry that it cannot be expressed. They went to all the waters in the world; vows, pilgrimages, all ways were tried, and all to no purpose.

At last, however, the Queen had a daughter. There was a very fine christening; and the Princess had for her god-mothers all the fairies they could find in the whole kingdom (they found seven), that every one of them might give her a gift, as was the custom of fairies in those days. By this means the Princess had all the perfections imaginable.

After the ceremonies of the christening were over, all the company returned to the King's palace, where was prepared a great feast for the fairies. But as they were all sitting down at table they saw come into the hall a very old fairy, whom they had not invited, because it was above fifty years since she had been out of a certain tower, and she was believed to be either dead or enchanted.

The King ordered her a cover, but could not furnish her with a case of gold as the others, because they had seven only made for the seven fairies. The old Fairy fancied she was slighted, and muttered some threats between her teeth. One of the young fairies who sat by her overheard how she grumbled; and, judging that she might give the little Princess some unlucky gift, went, as soon as they rose from the table, and hid herself behind the hangings, that she might speak last, and repair, as much as she could, the evil which the old Fairy might intend.

In the meanwhile all the fairies began to give their gifts to the Princess. The youngest gave her for a gift that she should be the most beautiful person in the world; the next, that she should have the wit of an angel; the third, that she should have a wonderful grace in everything she did; the fourth, that she should dance perfectly well; the fifth, that she should sing like a nightingale; and the sixth,

that she should play all kinds of music to the utmost perfection.

The old Fairy's turn coming next, with a head shaking more with spite than age, she said that the Princess should have her hand pierced with a spindle and die of the wound. This terrible gift made the whole company tremble, and everybody fell a-crying.

At the very instant the young Fairy came out from behind the hangings, and spake these words aloud:

"Assure yourselves, O King and Queen, that your daughter shall not die of this disaster. It is true, I have no power to undo entirely what my elder has done. The Princess shall indeed pierce her hand with a spindle; but, instead of dying, she shall only fall into a profound sleep, which shall last a hundred years, at the expiration of which a king's son shall come and awake her."

"The Sleeping Beauty in the Wood", from *The Blue Fairy Book* edited by Andrew Lang c. 1889.

A Child's Present

Go pretty child, and bear this flower
Unto thy little Saviour;
And tell Him, by that bud now blown,
He is the Rose of Sharon known:
When thou hast said so, stick it there
Upon His bib, or stomacher:
And tell Him (for good handsel too)
That thou hast brought a whistle new,
Made of a clean straight oaten reed,
To charm His cries (at time of need):
Tell Him, for coral, thou hast none;
But if thou hadst, He should have one;
But poor thou art, and known to be
Even as moneyless, as He.
Lastly, if thou canst win a kiss
From those mellifluous lips of His;
Then never take a second on,
To spoil the first impression.

Robert Herrick (1591-1674)

Christening Gifts

Salt, an egg, bread, matches and a silver coin were traditionally brought to a new baby, and it is still common for a baby to have its "palm crossed with silver" to ensure good fortune in later life. Christening presents from godparents have special significance and are often made from silver: traditional gifts include a spoon or mug for a boy and a bracelet or other jewellery for a girl.

A lovely nineteenth-century gift which could be copied today is the layette pincushion. This was a small, cream satin cushion, edged with lace or a frill, and filled with bran or sawdust. Pins were pushed in to spell out a message or create patterns of flowers and leaves. "Welcome little stranger" or "Bless the babe" were favourite greetings, and the date and place of birth were often included.

More functional pincushions were also popular as christening gifts, since everyone used pins all the time. Until the invention of the safety pin in 1878, clothes were fastened with straight pins, though some mothers prudently avoided this dangerous practice by actually sewing their babies into their day clothes each morning.

In Scotland the baby's shawl might be held together with a luckenbooth – a silver brooch in the shape of a heart and crown. This would have been given to the mother as a betrothal gift, and she would pin it to her children's shawls as a reminder of their parents' love. Shawls are another time-honoured baby gift, and the most beautiful are Shetland "wedding ring" shawls, knitted in single-ply wool, in intricate lace designs. They are so-called because the yarn is so gossamer-fine that the completed shawl can be passed through a wedding ring.

Coral has long been thought to have magic powers, and thick stems of it were used to make the handles of elaborate silver rattles. In the late eighteenth century, these silver rattle handles were hung with tiny silver bells to entertain the baby, as well as

Above: *A necklace of coral beads was often a child's first present, a custom that dates back to Roman times. The silver bear napkin ring, made in 1910, was a christening gift for an Edwardian child.*

to warn away bad spirits. In ancient Rome, mothers hung a string of coral beads on the side of a baby's cradle to "preserve and fasten the teeth", and it was also believed that it would protect the child against lightning strikes and shipwrecks.

Wrapping a newborn baby in its mother's smock was once thought to endow the child with her charm, while in Ireland a child's first garment was traditionally its father's shirt. It was hoped that this piece of adult clothing would protect the baby from

eerie fairies who were always on the lookout for healthy infants to swap for their changelings. These charming folk beliefs could be prettily echoed by making a patchwork quilt for the baby's crib, using old shirtings and dress prints.

Above: *A wonderful old teddy bear with his very own lacy bib would make a charming christening gift.*

Birthstones and Flowers

When choosing or making a gift for a newborn baby, a good source of appropriate colours and motifs can be found in traditional lists of birthstones and plants. The plants vary from country to country, but always have flowers that bloom during the birthday month. This list comes from 19th-century America.

MONTH	GEMSTONE	FLOWER
January	garnet	snowdrop
February	amethyst	primrose
March	jasper	violet
April	sapphire	daisy
May	emerald	hawthorn
June	agate	honeysuckle
July	turquoise	water lily
August	carnelian	poppy
September	chrysolite	morning glory
October	beryl	hops
November	topaz	chrysanthemum
December	ruby	holly

Embroidered Keepsake

For centuries an embroidered pincushion was a traditional part of the new baby's layette. This pretty little cushion, embroidered in cross-stitch with the baby's initial, could be put to practical use for holding pins, or filled with lavender or pot-pourri as a fragrant memento.

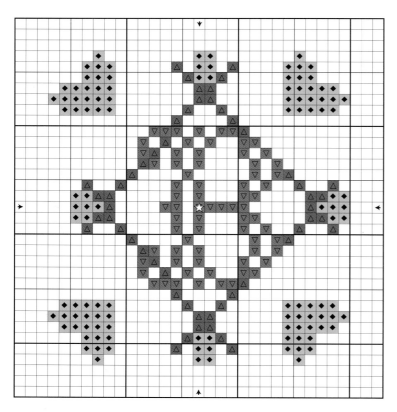

- 15cm/6in square 25 count evenweave cotton
- tacking (basting) thread
- needle
- embroidery hoop (frame)
- stranded embroidery thread (floss) in pale pink, pale green and red
- tapestry needle
- 118 small pink beads

- scissors
- 15cm/6in square white backing fabric
- sewing machine
- matching sewing thread
- two 14cm/5½in squares polyester wadding (batting)
- pins
- 75cm/30in white crocheted lace edging

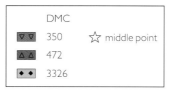

DMC		
▽▽	350	☆ middle point
▲▲	472	
◆◆	3326	

1 To work the cross-stitch, find the centre of the linen square and tack (baste) guidelines in both directions. Following the chart, work the cross-stitch using three strands of embroidery thread (floss) over two threads. Once the design is complete, sew a bead over the top of each stitch in the pink hearts. Use a double length of thread and begin with a secure knot.

2 To make up the cushion, trim away the excess fabric leaving a border of 4cm/1½in around the cross-stitch. Trim the backing fabric to match. Taking a 1cm/½in seam allowance, stitch the embroidery and backing fabric together with right sides facing, leaving a gap along one side. Trim the seams and across the corners, and turn through.

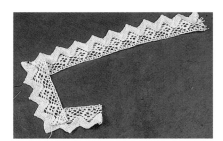

3 Tuck the wadding (batting) into the cushion and slip-stitch to close. Mitre the corners of the lace to fit by folding and stitching diagonally on the wrong side. Join the lace ends and pin to the cushion 1cm/½in in from the edge. Stitch in place.

Right: *If you want to give the cushion an antique look, dip the fabric in weak tea to colour it slightly.*

Harlequin Patchwork
Teddy

Soft toys, like this adorable satin bear, were often made from patchwork in days gone by. Using a traditional box design, make two rectangles of patchwork large enough to fit the bear pattern, then cut out the shape.

fold

- thin card (cardboard)
- pencil
- craft knife
- 50 x 90cm/20 x 36in iron-on interfacing
- scissors

- iron
- satin fabric scraps in assorted colours
- pins
- tacking (basting) thread
- sewing machine

- matching sewing thread
- needle
- polyester wadding (batting)

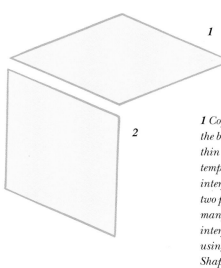

1

2

1 Copy the templates on this page, enlarging the bear to the size required, and cut out of thin card (cardboard). Use the patch templates to transfer the shapes to the interfacing. Cut out enough shapes for the two patchwork pieces. You will need twice as many patches in shape 2. Iron the interfacing shapes to the back of the satin, using one colour for all the shape 1 pieces. Shape 2 should be in assorted colours with an equal number in dark and light shades to achieve a three-dimensional effect. Cut out the shapes leaving a 5mm /¼ in seam allowance.

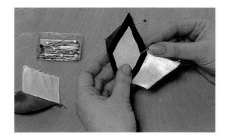

2 With right sides facing, join one light and one dark shape 2 to form the "box" sides. Pin shape 1 to the angled patch, matching the corners. Tack (baste) from the middle of the angle to the end of the seam. Match the second edge of shape 1 to the adjacent patch. Tack from the centre point to the other end.

3 Make up all the boxes, then stitch them together in horizontal rows. Stitch the rows together. Using the template, cut out two bear shapes in interfacing and iron to the wrong side of each patchwork. Cut out patchwork shapes around interfacing, adding a 1cm /½ in seam allowance. With right sides facing, stitch around the shape leaving a 5cm/2in gap. Clip into the corners, trim the seam and press. Turn through, fill with wadding (batting) and slip-stitch the gap.

Above: *Brightly contrasting colours and the appealing texture of satin will make this a much loved cuddly toy.*

Mossy Bear Candle holder

A candle is often presented to one of the baby's parents after the christening as a symbol of spiritual enlightenment, and this idea can be echoed in a more lighthearted way in the decorations for the christening party. An animal-shaped candle holder is especially appropriate, and would also make an original gift.

- fine-mesh chicken wire
- wire cutters
- candle
- carpet moss
- stub (floral) wires
- ribbon

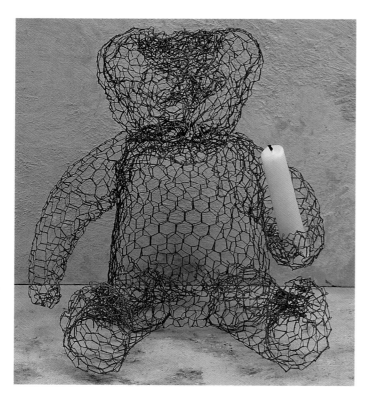

1 Cut a rectangle of chicken wire for the bear's head and torso. Bend it into a tube and secure by twisting the wire ends together. Push any sharp ends to the inside of the frame. About a third of the way down the tube, gather in the wire to form the neck. Join together and round off each end of the tube. Manipulate the head section to form the ears and nose.

2 Make the arms and legs separately from tubes of wire and join by twisting the wire ends on to the torso. Push the candle into one paw, bending the wire to give it a firm base which will hold it steady.

3 Lay carpet moss on top of the chicken wire and fix it in position using short lengths of stub (floral) wire bent into U-shaped staples. When the bear is completely covered, finish with a ribbon bow around the neck.

Right: *Animal-shaped candle holders appeal to both children and adults. Other animal shapes, such as rabbits or lambs, could be made in the same way for the christening party.*

Summer Christening Flowers

Flowers make a lovely gift for the baby's parents on the day of the christening, and they will be hugely appreciated if they are already prettily arranged. The delicacy of these flowers, including double tulips, ranunculus, phlox and spray roses, makes an appropriate arrangement for the occasion.

- florist's foam block
- kitchen knife
- small galvanized metal bucket
- 1 bunch pittosporum

- scissors
- 15 stems pale pink 'Angelique' tulips
- 5 stems white spray roses
- 10 stems white ranunculus

- 10 stems white phlox
- 1 bunch dried lavender
- ribbon

1 Soak the florist's foam in water, cut it to fit the bucket and wedge it firmly in place. Cut the pittosporum to a length of 12cm/4½in and clean the leaves from the lower part of the stems. Push the stems into the foam to create a domed foliage outline for the arrangement.

2 Cut the tulip stems to a length of 10cm/4in and distribute them evenly throughout the foliage. Cut individual shoots from the main stems of the spray roses to a length of 10cm/4in, and arrange throughout the display, using full blooms at the centre and buds around the edge.

3 Cut the ranunculus and phlox stems to a length of 10cm/4in and distribute both throughout the display. Cut the lavender stems to a length of 12cm/4½in and arrange in groups among the flowers and foliage. Tie the ribbon around the rim of the bucket and finish in a generous bow.

Right: *The soft, subtle colours of the flowers are suitable for a baby boy or girl, and the scent of the phlox and lavender is an added bonus.*

Planted Flower Basket

Plant up a wire basket with delicate cyclamen and deliciously scented lily of the valley to make a beautiful and long-lasting baby gift that provides the perfect finishing touch to any nursery.

- wire basket
- Spanish moss
- cellophane (plastic wrap)
- scissors
- 3 pots miniature white cyclamen
- 3 pots lily of the valley
- paper ribbon

1 Line the wire basket generously with handfuls of Spanish moss, then carefully line the moss with cellophane (plastic wrap). Trim the cellophane level with the rim of the basket.

2 Remove the plants from their pots. Loosen the soil and the roots a little before arranging them in the basket, alternating the cyclamen with the lily of the valley.

3 Make sure that the plants are firmly embedded in the basket. Make two small bows from the paper ribbon and attach one to the rim on each side of the basket at the base of the handle.

Right: *The combination of two plants with simple, miniature white flowers – baby cyclamen and lily of the valley – makes a design of charm and purity, perfect for a tiny baby.*

Lucky Horseshoe
Present

What could be nicer for new parents than to receive a floral symbol of good luck on the day of their baby's christening? The whites and pale green of this dried-flower horseshoe will make it a lovely decoration for the nursery and an ideal memento of a happy occasion.

- 14 heads dried white roses
- 60 heads dried phalaris grass
- 42 heads dried honesty
- scissors
- fine and medium florist's wire
- florist's (stem-wrap) tape
- ribbon

1 Cut all the stems to a length of about 2.5cm/1in. Using fine florist's wire, mount the roses individually, the phalaris grass in groups of five and the honesty in clusters of three stems. Bind each wired stem with florist's (stem-wrap) tape.

2 Bind three 30cm/12in lengths of medium florist's wire together using florist's (stem-wrap) tape to form a stay wire for the horseshoe shape.

3 Form three small ribbon bows about 4cm/1½in wide and bind them at their centres with fine florist's wire. Cut a 30cm/12in length of ribbon and bind each end with fine wire to form the handle for the horseshoe.

4 *Bend the stay wire into a horseshoe shape. Tape one wired end of the ribbon to one end of the stay wire and tape one of the bows over the join.*

5 *Starting at the bow, tape the flowers to the wire in a repeating sequence of phalaris, rose and honesty. When you reach the centre, add a second bow. Tape the other end of the ribbon handle and the final bow to the other end and work the flowers in the same sequence back to the centre.*

Right: *A gift of dried flowers will last indefinitely and will be treasured as a good luck token by the parents and the growing child.*

CHRISTENING GOWN

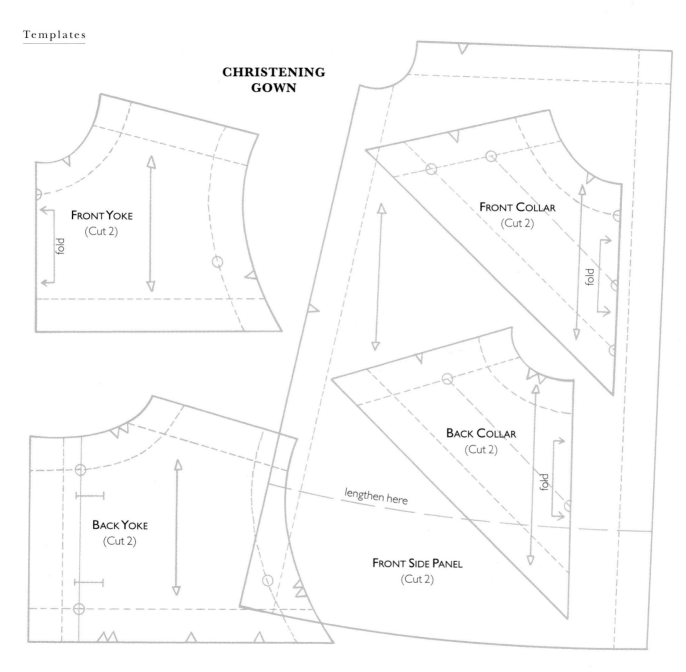

FRONT YOKE
(Cut 2)

fold

FRONT COLLAR
(Cut 2)

fold

BACK YOKE
(Cut 2)

BACK COLLAR
(Cut 2)

fold

lengthen here

FRONT SIDE PANEL
(Cut 2)

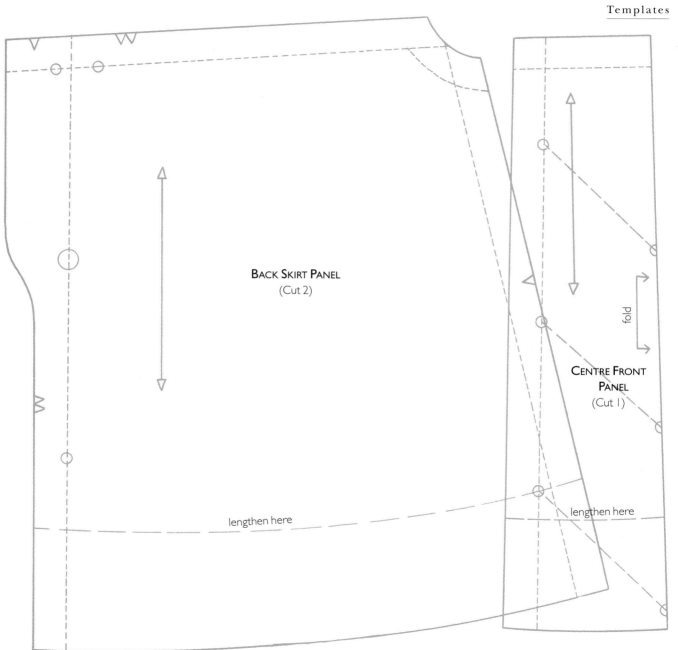

BACK SKIRT PANEL
(Cut 2)

CENTRE FRONT
PANEL
(Cut 1)

fold

lengthen here

lengthen here

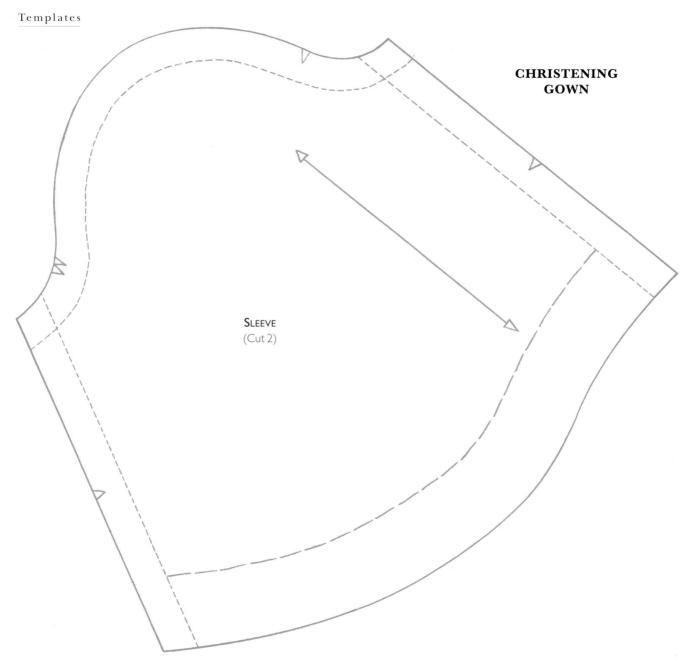

CHRISTENING GOWN

SLEEVE
(Cut 2)

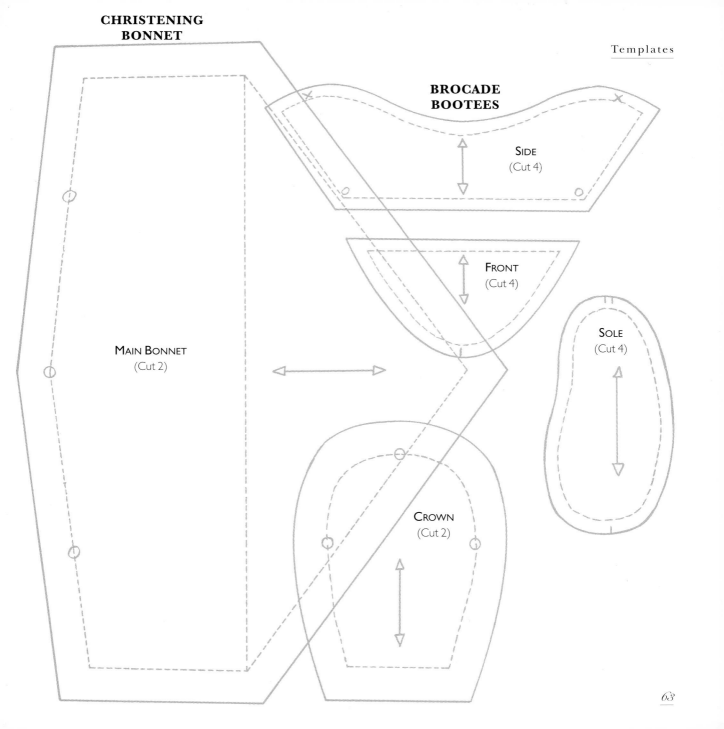

CHRISTENING BONNET

BROCADE BOOTEES

SIDE
(Cut 4)

FRONT
(Cut 4)

SOLE
(Cut 4)

MAIN BONNET
(Cut 2)

CROWN
(Cut 2)

Index and acknowledgements

Picture Acknowledgements

The Publishers thank the following agencies for permission to use their pictures:

The Bridgeman Art Library:York City Art Gallery p6; Josef Mensing Gallery p40.

Edimedia: Musée Petiet/P Cartier p9; Private collection p14/15; Private collection p18; Bridgeman Art Library p20; Private collection p44.

E. T. Archive: p43.

Fine Art Photographic Library Limited: Waterhouse & Dodd p7; Haynes Fine Art p8; Courtesy of Mr Fulda p10; Private collections p11; p12; p15; p19; p21; p41; p45.